HONORING
Our Ancestors

Stories and Pictures
by Fourteen Artists

Edited by Harriet Rohmer

Children's Book Press
San Francisco, California

HONO

 **I**'ve been thinking for a while now that as we approach a new millennium, it's time to look back at where we've been and to honor those who came before us—our ancestors. So I talked to some of the artists I've worked with. They were very excited about the idea. Then I talked to some artists who I hadn't worked with, but whose work I had admired for years. They were excited, too. That is how this book came to be.

Honoring Our Ancestors is a picture book by fourteen outstanding artists, honoring the ancestors who most influenced their lives. Some of these ancestors are family members. Others are ancestors in spirit. Some are still alive today. Others lived hundreds of years ago. They are African, African American, Chinese, Filipino,

RING *Our Ancestors*

Jewish, Lebanese, Mexican, Mexican American, Native American, and Puerto Rican—important people who usually don't make it into the history books. They're the heart and soul of who we are as a people.

I hope that this book will inspire children to talk to their elders, to honor their own ancestors, and to learn respect for other people's ancestors.

—*Harriet Rohmer*

Harriet Rohmer is the Publisher and Executive Director of Children's Book Press in San Francisco, California, the pioneering nonprofit organization she founded in 1975.

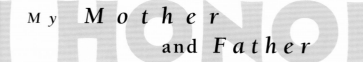

I HONOR

My *Mother* and *Father*

Trinidad Angel and
Carlos Angel

CARL ANGEL

My parents' stories are like hot cocoa on a cold night. They warm me up and comfort me. Mom tells me stories about her dreams and superstitions. I remember her story of Bangus, the milkfish. If he swims into your dreams, it means good fortune the next day.

Dad tells me stories of real-life adventure. I'd imagine him as a boy during World War II dodging enemy bombs in the Philippines, or later on, as a sailor in the U.S. Navy, traveling to strange new places.

That's Dad in the sun and Mom in the moon, and me in between, riding the milkfish. The words are from my Mom's stories.

Mom's stories helped her believe in her dreams. Dad's stories helped him trust his adventurous spirit. Through their stories, I've grown to believe in both. When I paint, their worlds of dreams and adventure flow through me, and my own colorful story begins!

Carl Angel is a painter and illustrator whose work is exhibited in galleries and museums throughout the San Francisco Bay Area. He was born in Bainbridge, Maryland, in 1968, raised in Hawaii, and now lives in Oakland, California.

I HONOR

My *Father* and M o t h e r

Enrique Chagoya Galicia and
Ofelia Flores de Chagoya

Enrique Chagoya

I dedicate this drawing to my parents because they were my most important source of love and support when I was growing up.

My father gave me my first drawing and painting lessons and taught me color theory when I was seven years old. I remember that when I first saw him drawing landscapes and animals I thought his hand was magical. Ever since then I've always wanted to do the same thing.

My mother had a big heart, not only for our family, but for many people who knew her. She went out of her way to help people in need and never expected anything back.

I drew the shape of my mother's body using the words "nunca me digas adios." That's Spanish for "never tell me good-bye." She never wanted to say good-bye to me when I left Mexico. Instead, she said, "See you later." When she died four years ago, we told each other, "See you later."

Enrique Chagoya teaches painting, drawing, and printmaking at Stanford University. His paintings and graphics are shown in museums and galleries throughout the world. He was born in Mexico City in 1953, moved to the San Francisco Bay Area in 1979, and now lives in San Francisco, California.

George Crespo

This is my grandfather, Abuelo Antonio. (*Abuelo* means "grandfather" in Spanish.) He lived on a farm in Puerto Rico. I painted him holding a traditional planting stick and releasing seeds into the ground. He loved working with plants. I am next to Abuelo, looking up at a hawk. When I was a child there was a hawk that followed me everywhere, even in my dreams.

You can see four tuber vegetables, like the ones Abuelo farmed. These vegetables were left to us by the Tainos, our indigenous Puerto Rican ancestors.

George Crespo is an illustrator, a sculptor, an author, and a teacher. He was born in Yonkers, New York, in 1962, and moved back and forth with his family between Puerto Rico and New York. He now lives in the Bronx in New York City.

At the bottom of the painting is an underground river that ran under the farm. Since the beginning of time the river has been carving out huge underground caves. Not long ago I went to visit the river. The land above it belongs to the government now. It no longer belongs to my family. At first I was sad, but then I realized that when I am quiet, I can feel the river running inside me. It lives in me, just like my grandparents and my Taino ancestors.

My *Ancestor*

Abba Moses the Black

MARK DUKES

Mark Dukes is an iconographer and painter. He is working on an icon mural of 75 dancing saints for St. Gregory's Episcopal Church in San Francisco. Mark was born in Columbus, Ohio, in 1958 and now lives in Oakland, California.

My spiritual ancestor, Abba Moses the Black, lived 1,600 years ago. He used to be the leader of a gang of thieves. One day, while he was hiding from the law, he met a group of monks who lived simple, prayerful lives in the deserts of Egypt. He decided to join them.

In my picture he is talking to his gang about his newfound experience of joy in doing good. The thieves on the left drop their knives and decide to change their lives. The thieves on the right haven't decided yet. Later, they will drop their weapons, change their violent lives, and follow their leader, Abba Moses.

I'm one of the gang. Can you find me? Instead of a knife, I have a paintbrush. It's the magic of my paintbrush that enables me to travel back in time.

Above us are two more saints. Tekla Haymanot is a legendary Ethiopian saint. Mahatma Gandhi is an Indian saint who lived in modern times. I put him with Tekla because I thought Gandhi would like a ride on a magic carpet of light. Wouldn't you?

I HONOR

My Great-Grandmother
Refugio Morales

Maya Christina Gonzalez

My great-grandmother Refugio may have been a *curandera*—a traditional healer who made her own medicines from plants and herbs. I met her only once, when I was very young. I don't know much about her life, but she has always inspired me. This is the way I imagine her telling her story:

Maya Christina Gonzalez is an artist and illustrator whose work is shown in many galleries. She loves to work in the schools, teaching children about art. Maya was born in Lancaster, California, in 1964 and now lives in San Francisco, California.

I am Refugio. I was born in 1898 in the heart of Mexico. People call me the "Galloping Curandera" because I ride through the desert on my horse to do my healing work. When someone is sick, I don't listen to their words as much as I listen to their hearts and their bodies. Then I gallop into the desert to find the perfect plant to help them get better.

In the desert, I listen to the voices of the plants. They call out my name and tell me their healing stories. That is how I learned to be a curandera—by listening to things you think have no voice. This is my joy, so this is my work.

I HONOR

My Grandmother

Alease Lucas Henry

Caryl Henry

Have you ever noticed the amazing ways in which Black women style their hair?

Braids Curls Ponytails Afros Buns of all shapes and sizes!

My grandmother, Nana Henry (pictured center), was a cosmetologist. Nana moved to New York's Harlem in 1916, and learned how to straighten, style and care for Black hair at Madame C.J. Walker's School of Beauty Culture.

She fried it, she dyed it, she really combed and styled it!

Madame Walker (pictured left) was the first Black woman millionaire, establishing "beauty culture" schools all over the United States. She trained hundreds of women in the business of beauty and self-care.

When I was little, the women in my family were really into doing my hair. I didn't like it! All that hot combing, perming and pulling was no fun! I respect my Nana and Madame C.J. Walker, but as soon as I was able, I threw away my combs and went natural with dread-locks (pictured right). Now my head is nappy—oops, I mean happy!

Caryl Henry is a painter and mixed-media artist who is deeply influenced by the art of the Yoruba people of West Africa. She was born in New Brunswick, New Jersey, in 1955 and now lives in Oakland, California.

My *Father*

Fook Tow Hom

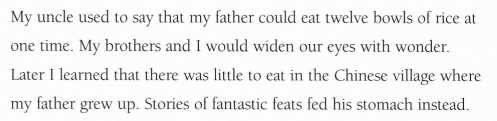

Nancy Hom

My uncle used to say that my father could eat twelve bowls of rice at one time. My brothers and I would widen our eyes with wonder. Later I learned that there was little to eat in the Chinese village where my father grew up. Stories of fantastic feats fed his stomach instead.

My father came to America on a big ship. He was scared and didn't know what lay ahead of him. He worked in a Chinese restaurant, politely serving food and cleaning dishes. But behind the soft smile he was Guan Gong, the mighty warrior, the god of martial arts and scholars in Chinese folklore. "He can wrestle a tiger with one hand," said my uncle in a deep whisper. "Just feel his muscles." We reached out to touch the arms that were hard from lifting huge plates of food and marveled.

That is the way I remember my father and all the people who came from China to seek their fortunes—brave, strong, facing a new land with the spirit of Guan Gong to guide their way.

Nancy Hom is an artist, mother, designer, and executive director of an Asian American arts organization. She was born in Toisan, China, in 1949 and grew up in New York City. She now lives in San Francisco with her photographer husband, Bob Hsiang, and their daughter, Nicole.

My Grandmother

Wang Ju-shou

Hung Liu

Hung Liu is an internationally exhibited painter who often explores themes of Chinese women in history. Born in Changchun, China, in 1948, she came to the United States in 1984, and now lives in Oakland, California.

Many years ago in China, my grandmother made shoes for our family. Her shoes were very comfortable—cool in summer, warm in winter.

I used to love to watch my grandmother make shoes. She would gather pieces of old clothes and used fabric, paint them with a creamy flour paste, and then layer them on a flat wooden board to dry. The changing colors and patterns of the fabric were beautiful to watch. Soon, the fabric became a strong, sturdy sheet, and she would cut pieces of it to form the shoes. Sometimes she would even let me be her little helper!

I was amazed by every cut and snip and fold. Watching her was like watching a master artist. She made all her decisions on the spot. I was proud of my grandmother because she used faded old clothes to make colorful new shoes.

Although her own feet had been bound and it was hard for her to walk, my grandmother devoted herself to making beautiful shoes for the next generations.

My Great-Grandmother

Wilis-Kol-Kold

Judith Lowry

My great-grandmother, Wilis-Kol-Kold, was an Indian woman of the Pit-River tribe of northern California.

When she was a child she became very ill, and everyone thought she had died. In those days the Indians buried people on scaffolds. Wilis-Kol-Kold was put on her scaffold, but in a couple of days she awoke and cried for her mother. The people were so surprised and happy to see her alive! They believed she had visited the world of the spirits. As she grew up, she was trained to be a healer. People came to her when they were sick, and she made them better.

When my father was a boy he would help her fetch water and wood. She would tell him wonderful Indian stories about the time when the animals could talk. My father passed her stories on to me. I passed them on to my children, and now they pass them on to their children. That is the way it has always been, and, I hope, will always be.

Judith Lowry, of Mountain Maidu, Hamawi Pit-River, and Australian descent, is one of California's premiere contemporary Native American artists. She was born in Washington, D.C., in 1948 and now lives in Nevada City, California.

Stephen Von Mason

To our ancestors: May their spirits live forever. Let us always remember them by naming our children after them and researching our history, so that those who follow us may also know their heritage.
—Katherine Mae Mason-Chavis (my aunt)

This painting is for my ancestors. On the left is my great-great-great-grandfather, Pharoah Jackson Chesney. He was a pioneer—one of the first settlers of Knoxville, Tennessee. He lived to be 120 years old.

On the right is my uncle, Jordan Douglass Chavis, Jr. He was a famous musician, the leader of a big band called "The Tennessee Collegians" from Tennessee State University. He was a musical pioneer. He started Tennessee State's music department.

In the center is my father, Cornelius Grant Mason, Jr., in the clothes he wore when he was a student pilot in the late 1940s. He, too, was a pioneer—part of the first group of Black pilots in America.

Stephen Von Mason is a painter, printmaker, and fine art framer whose work is exhibited internationally. He was born in South Bend, Indiana, in 1954 and now lives in Oakland, California.

1998

SYMASON

Jordan-Douglass "Chick" Chavis Jr.

...Played...Carnegie Hall alongside...Billie Holiday and Lester Young...

Cornelius Grant Mason Jr.

...A Student Pilot...

Henry McClaren...Leola Carter...

PARENTS

Cornelius Grant Mason Jr.
- m. Josephine Beechum-Mason...Deceased
- m. Loistean Mason Ed.D.

AUNTS and UNCLES

Jordan Douglass Chavis Jr. | Ervin Edward Mason
Katherine M. Mason-Chavis | Angie Snodgrass-Mason

GREAT GRANDPARENTS

Tip Chesney and Uretha B. McFeeter-Chesney

GREAT, GREAT, GREAT Grandparents

Isaac Burke and Amanda Sharp-Burke
...was a Blacksmith from Algiers, Algeria-N. Afric
Pharoah Jackson and Orie Chesney

I HONOR

My
Ancestors

Mira Reisberg

These are my ancestors. Some of them are my blood relatives. Others are my relatives in spirit. All of them helped make me who I am today.

♥ My parents: they gave me life, confidence, a love of language, laughter, and Jewish ritual.

♥ My grandparents (three of them killed in the Holocaust): I know so little about them.

♥ The Kouri (Aboriginal) people from Australia, my birthland: their art and rituals inspire me.

♥ Albert Einstein: eccentric, brilliant, kind.

♥ Frida Kahlo: fabulous, courageous Mexican artist.

♥ Groucho Marx: very funny actor and comedian.

♥ Marc Chagall: fanciful, soulful painter of topsy-turvy worlds.

♥ Gertrude Stein and Alice B. Toklas: Gertrude wrote a new kind of writing. Alice made it possible.

♥ Hannah Senesh: beautiful, brave Jewish poet and Resistance fighter, killed in the Holocaust.

These are my ancestors. I honor and thank them.

Mira Reisberg is an artist, designer, illustrator, and art teacher who loves to create art projects with children. She was born in Melbourne, Australia, in 1953 and now lives in San Francisco, California.

My *Three Aunts*

Edna, Viney, and Grace Mannings

JoeSam.

When I think about my ancestors, I think of the three aunts who raised me in Harlem during the 1940s. Edna, Viney, and Grace were maids who worked in the white neighborhoods of Manhattan. Originally from Trinidad, they hated the hard, gray landscape of New York City—especially during the cold winters.

My aunts draped themselves in the most colorful clothing they could find. Even in the dead of winter they would wear bright turbans or embellish their hats with colorful scraps. They brought the warmth of Africa and the West Indies to Harlem.

My aunts' bright clothing created a halo of light around them; that's why I show them against a background of deep, golden yellow. Each portrait uses a different medium—watercolor, pastel crayon, and collage. The collage above them evokes the mood of Africa and the Caribbean, and shows how Edna, Viney, and Grace carried their heritage with them wherever they went.

JoeSam. is a mixed-media artist with a strong love of Third World cultures. Known for his innovative public art sculptures, he is also an internationally recognized painter. He was born in Harlem, New York, in 1939 and now lives in San Francisco, California.

Patssi Valdez

Every morning I used to watch my mom get ready for her workday. I watched her put on makeup, lipstick and her favorite cologne. She always made sure she looked her best. She would leave when it was still dark outside and walk to the bus stop to go to work at Sears.

We lived on Record Street in East L.A. My parents were divorced, and my mom worked hard to care for me and my sister. Sometimes I felt sad because she had to leave us alone. But if she hadn't gone to work, we wouldn't have had a place to live.

Years later, my mom put herself through school and started her own business. She gave me the courage to be independent, hardworking, and honest.

This is a painting of my mom's room, but I didn't put her in the picture. Instead I painted her things, and her shadow in the mirror. I wanted to show how I felt her presence in the room even when she wasn't there.

Patssi Valdez, a leading figure in the Chicano art movement, is a painter and a set and costume designer for theater, film, and television. She lives in Los Angeles, California, where she was born in 1951.

I HONOR

My *Grandmother*

Miriam Sultani Zughaib

Helen Zughaib

This is Teta, my Lebanese grandmother. (*Teta* means "grandmother" in Arabic.) She grew up in Syria and Lebanon and came to America after World War II. The man in the picture frame is Teta's husband, my grandfather. When I was a child I loved going to Teta's house—it was so warm and always smelled delicious. Teta would pinch my cheek and say, "I love you, I love you, I love you!"

Scraps of cloth, thread and yarn were everywhere. Teta was a wonderful seamstress. The clothes she made were beautiful and so unusual that you never knew what she would put together. I learned about colors and patterns from Teta.

She would sit with me for hours, teaching me how to knit and crochet. While we were knitting, she would share stories about her childhood. She was an educated woman, which was very unusual in those days. She often advised me to "put education in your heart, not boys!" Well, thanks to you, Teta, I put art in my heart, too.

Helen Zughaib is a painter whose work is shown in many galleries in the metropolitan D.C. area. She was born in Beirut, Lebanon, in 1959 and now lives in Washington, D.C., with her two cats, Noodle and Chunky Beef.

HONORING OUR ANCESTORS:
Stories and Pictures by Fourteen Artists

Carl Angel (pp. 4-5)
Medium: acrylics
Photo of artist: Carl Angel

Enrique Chagoya (pp. 6-7)
Medium: pencil and acrylics on paper
Photo of artist: Dorothy Alexander

George Crespo (pp. 8-9)
Medium: oil paint on burlap; frame is cedo wood and twine
Photo of artist: Nelson Bakerman
Photo of ancestor: George Crespo

Mark Dukes (pp. 10-11)
Medium: acrylics on canvas
Photo of artist: David Singer
Painting of ancestor: Mark Dukes

Maya Christina Gonzalez (pp. 12-13)
Medium: acrylics on paper
Photo of artist: Wendi Raw

Caryl Henry (pp. 14-15)
Medium: mixed-media
Photo of artist: André Kreft
Photo of ancestor: Wilmore Henry

Nancy Hom (pp. 16-17)
Medium: gouache
Photo of artist: Bob Hsiang

Hung Liu (pp. 18-19)
Medium: water-based media
Photo of artist: Mitchell Kearney
Photo of ancestor: Hung Liu

Judith Lowry (pp. 20-21)
Medium: acrylics on canvas
Photo of artist: Lia Groeling

Stephen Von Mason (pp. 22-23)
Medium: oil on rag paper
Photo of artist: Tony Smith

Mira Reisberg (pp. 24-25)
Medium: acrylics and mixed-media
Photo of artist: Georgia Ryan

JoeSam. (pp. 26-27)
Medium: mixed-media
Photo of artist: Michael Jang

Pattsi Valdez (pp. 28-29)
Medium: gouache
Photo of artist: Vern Evans

Helen Zughaib (pp. 30-31)
Medium: gouache and ink on board
Photo of artist: Lina Dajani Malas

Consulting Editor: David Schecter   Design and Production: Cathleen O'Brien   Editorial/Production Assistant: Laura Atkins

Thanks to the staff of Children's Book Press: Emily Romero, Stephanie Sloan, Christina Tarango, and Saba Waheed.

Children's Book Press is a nonprofit publisher of multicultural literature for children, supported in part by grants from the California Arts Council. Write us for a complimentary catalog: Children's Book Press, 2211 Mission Street, San Francisco, CA 94110, (415) 821-3080, cbookpress@cbookpress.org

Distributed to the book trade by Publishers Group West
Quantity discounts available through the publisher for educational and nonprofit use.

Library of Congress Cataloging-in-Publication Data
Honoring our ancestors: pictures and stories by fourteen artists; edited by Harriet Rohmer. pm cm. Summary: Fourteen artists and picture book illustrators present paintings with descriptions of ancestors who have inspired them. ISBN 0-89239-158-8 1. Minority artists—United States—Psychology—Juvenile literature. 2. Minorities in art—Juvenile literature. N6537.5.H66 1999 759.13—DC21 98-38686 CIP AC

Printed in Hong Kong by Marwin Productions
10 9 8 7 6 5 4 3 2